Sitting in Lawn Chairs
After a Complicated Day

Sitting in Lawn Chairs
After a Complicated Day

Marg Walker

NODIN PRESS

ACKNOWLEDGEMENTS

I would like to thank the editors of journals who have published many of these poems over the last twenty years; my many writing partners, first readers and teachers, principally Deborah Keenan, for their support and critique, and for sharing with me their love of poetry's power and grace; this vibrant community of poets, organizations, bookstores, and reading venues for making Minnesota a place where poetry flourishes; Morgan Grayce Willow, for her steadfast encouragement and coaching as I transformed my mound of poems into a book; Norton Stillman, for loving the language of poems and saying "yes" to these; my family, who believed in this book before I was able to; and all those who appear in these poems, unnamed but wholly loved. You know who you are.

A complete list of publication acknowledgements can be found on page 81.

I am grateful to composers Carol Barnett, Kelly Krebs, Libby Larsen, and Tim Takach for elevating some of my poems into beautiful music for vocal performance.

Book design and cover art: John Toren
Author portrait: Lesley Hauser

9 8 7 6 5 4 3 2 1

ISBN: 978-1-947237-25-4
Library of Congress Control Number: 2020930793

Nodin Press, LLC
5114 Cedar Lake Road
Minneapolis, MN
55416

www.nodinpress.com

for Eric, and for Jonathan

Contents

An Introduction to the Languages of Love

3   Sitting in Lawn Chairs After a Complicated Day
4   First Winter
6   What the Colt Knows
7   Photograph
8   How the Swedes Eat Grapefruit
9   What There Is to Remember
10   On the Water
11   The Heart

In Your Own Hands

15   Belated Thank-You Note to Myself
16   The Kind of Thing We Did
17   Potato Man
18   The Warm Lap of September
19   After I Left You, You Mentioned That You Loved Me
20   This New Arrangement
21   Cathedral Hill
22   At the Grocery
24   if you must begin again
25   This City of Your Choosing
26   Since My Return from Nicaragua
28   This May Not Be Correct
29   Half a World Away
30   When We Found Out About the Baby
31   Late Afternoon, Gulls

32   Bright Room with Linoleum Floor, 1993

33   It Will End Like This

34   Like the Bird

35   In Your Own Hands

Synchronizing the Heart

39   The Heart Wants You

40   The Art of Long Affection

41   Wide Open

42   Covenant

43   Absence

44   Aunt Grace

46   Draft a Little Something

47   Young Son, Sandwich Half-Eaten

48   You Will Recall with Fondness Your Fifties

49   The Ones She Seeks

51   Someone's Grandmother Picks Up the Mail

52   Mary Lou's Kitchen

54   Un-doing

55   Into Your Singular Room

57   Every Kind of Cloud

58   She Wakes Me to See Fireflies

59   Rocket Pajamas

60   Cliff Notes from Your Mother as You Leave Home

61   Terminal One

62   Letter to My Nieces

63   In the Beijing Alley Near Our Hotel

64   Suspended in the Air of China

65   Fishing Boats, Yangtze

67   Returning Home

68   Precipitous

70   Just Out of Reach

72   I Push Her Wheelchair in the City of My Childhood

73   A Quiet Hour

74   Cathy in My Room Last Night, Singing

75   Last Words

76   Blessing

77   What the Painter Dared Imagine

78   Varied and Marvelous Things

81   Acknowledgements

82   About the Author

1

*An Introduction
to the Languages
of Love*

SITTING IN LAWN CHAIRS AFTER A COMPLICATED DAY

Tonight's moon is a slim perfection,
a dangle of silver sliding across the world as it is.
Each tree below rustles a story,
reaching for heaven in its own way.
    Here in the back yard
our truths are rough as bark,
each one perfect as the incomplete moon.
With so much we cannot see
who am I to ask you to be anything more
than who you are?

There is no one you need to be for me.
No one you need to be
    for me.

First Winter

My parents had enough
to live on: their own bungalow
by then, a Chevy, a snow shovel,
a sidewalk leading away.
Into this small home I came
with my ravishing shock of dark hair,
impossible not to love –
I'm guessing here –
despite the timing.
My sister cradled me on her tiny lap
and petted me, lodging in her heart
a life-long need for dogs.
My brother dropped me one day
but not on my head.
I cannot say
if it was an accident.
I can say money was tight.
I can say my mother counted
among her blessings
the cloth diapers already bunched
in the drawer, the hand-me-down
clothes passed among friends.
Her mother, not yet dying,
helped with the laundry sometimes.
My mother, not yet formally depressed,
tended us the best she could
while my father earned our living.
How deep was the snow that year?
Did she sometimes sit while
my sister and brother napped

that first winter, rocking me and
smoothing my dark and silken brow?
I picture her
looking out at falling snow,
the yard asleep, its creatures
concealed in their burrows,
the sheath of fresh snow
not yet broken.

WHAT THE COLT KNOWS

Something the colt knows
within the hour of pushing
firm-hoofed and wet into the world
makes him unwrinkle his narrow legs
to stand for himself. Into the light
of quilted pastures he walks
at the flank of the mare
      alone.

Your mother claims
you tugged the bottle from her hands
at six months old, insistent
on feeding yourself. Relieved,
she let you be. You already knew
what the colt knows, your soft eyes
following her movements
      away.

PHOTOGRAPH

You stand before the mirror holding me
to your cheek, my blanket bunched
against your flowered dress. My eyes
are bright, adoring, as daughters all begin.

This is a time before memory, when being held
was enough, a time before I knew of words
and needed them. But here it is in grainy black and white:
you loved me too, and just as helplessly.

If only you had not been so afraid to lose
yourself in us, I think you would have found
– oh beloved field general –
our terms of surrender dear.

Turning toward me in the end, you asked me
to guard your unprotected flank, take care
of death's details, then find my own way home.
It must be here, in these old photographs

for even as I gave you what you asked
you would not speak of love, a thing
too holy to be reduced to words (was it?)
too intimate and strange for comfort (yes).

How the Swedes Eat Grapefruit

After his surgery my father asked her
to cut around the grapefruit wedges,
free each triangle from the membrane
so he could slip it pink and sweet
onto the breakfast spoon, no struggle.

I've always preferred to eat it that way,
he said. Knife poised, my mother stared.
You've never mentioned it to me
in fifty-seven years.

No. His lineage is of quiet men
who, undeterred by hardship,
since long before his Swedish grandmother
learned to live without complaint

no matter what the fare.
But this new line of thought today unspools:
claim what matters. Name the falsely fixed.
Ask now, he thinks, *ask now.*

WHAT THERE IS TO REMEMBER

In the darkened bathroom the candle flame
lures us with its slender light. I perch
on the edge of the tub and read to you
of wizards and adventurers
in whose noble quest each evening
you enlist. At five, you are a specialist
in the brotherhood of baths and books.

Lounging in bubbles, you lift your knees
into snow-covered mountains.
Wall shadows shift, a forest flickering
beyond our campfire. At a daring rescue
you burst upright, ease down again
to grieve the suffering
of an injured creature. Tonight

you asked for candlelight –
an adventure of our own making –
and I supplied it
as readily as any instruction
for what may lie ahead unseen,
my voice in the dark your touchstone,
steadfast as the pull of the page.

This is what there is to remember.
This is your mother, reading.

ON THE WATER

Lulled by the light
        lapping against the bow

the muffled flurry of birds
        in shoreline shrubs

the long   breath
        of feathered pines

you become true
        to your first nature

speechless   and primitive
        attuned   purely

to what the lake offers
        what the lake   withholds

The Heart

A helium balloon the first time
    slipping upward into impossible blue.

Next time
    a kite.

Fistfuls of perennial he-loves-me-
    he-loves-me-not; pitiful, really.

The currency
    of a spendthrift God.

Work boots and, every now and then,
    dancing shoes.

Fingertips and also
    fingerprints.

What I once dreamed that you,
    repulsed, held dripping from your hand.

Pepper spray
    sometimes.

A cello
    solo.

String theory, which is a candidate for the theory
    of everything, which nobody understands.

2

In Your Own Hands

BELATED THANK-YOU NOTE TO MYSELF

You didn't have much
money. Laughed about that.
Refused full time work and lived
on seven grand a year
so you could bike the parkways
any afternoon you pleased
beneath the arched branches
green as you were.
Wore work boots from Sears,
shit kickers you called them
'cause you weren't gonna take
none of that. For a night out
you'd ride the 14E downtown
past store windows whose luster
was nothing to your own shining.
Lie down on the cool cement
of a parking ramp's empty
top level. Eat fresh pineapple,
juice dribbling to your ears.
Consider the convivial stars.

THE KIND OF THING WE DID

I was new in the city and looking
for shared rent, not entanglement.
But she had lived a while alone
so the first time I brought home
groceries and in the morning
there was jam for toast
she cried.

Such a simple act she said
keeps you from the edge.

I knew nothing of edges then
and hadn't meant to learn –
it was just the kind of thing we did
in our twenties: chat with a stranger
in the park, play with her rumpled dog,
move in. Later, move away.
It wasn't supposed to be
chapter one of anything.

Still, I wonder if I should have
foreseen what was to come
from the anxious fluttering of her hands.
When do we become responsible
for one another? I remember her
odd, persistent gloom, her fragility
choking our small rooms
with tendrils of need too dense to part
except by cutting.

POTATO MAN

When we were poor,
you stole a potato from the co-op
and made it seem funny,
flourishing it from your pocket
like a magician.

On nights you couldn't sleep
you swam across the darkened lake
alone, or rode a bicycle without brakes
down the alley's graveled slope
past the rejected cats

out under the collapsing moon.
This daring made good stories
and we told more and more,
some of them made up,
each one true.

How necessary it was

to be together, to hide from grief
with one another. We gave everything
freely into each other's hands
so that ours could again
be empty.

The Warm Lap of September

The high meadow
of finch and thistle
     glows

in the amber hour
when the deer return

There is no one else
     for miles

Dusk is opening
its sketchbook

Wind fingers
the grasses
like shimmering
     piano keys

Into the feathering sky
thoughts drift
     like milkweed

until there is
nothing left
but this –

     at last
     just being

After I Left You, You Mentioned That You Loved Me

Not the Van Morrison album we played
obsessively, or the mattress on your floor,
its loamy scent redolent of rain. Not
the phenomenon of the Hennepin Avenue café
open at 3 a.m. when we needed pie, or
the cricket song that night you drove me home
because (over-served) I couldn't find reverse.
Not the summer concert under the parliament
of oaks, or the bud vase for my birthday,
one bubble trapped in the seclusion of glass.
Not the road trip through farm country,
the tent, the cows, a walk along
the Kickapoo in the buzzing sun.

In the end, nothing
made up for the lack of those three words,
how their long absence took on meaning,
how I'd needed them
like signposts to keep me going
out where the marked roads disappear.

This New Arrangement

I pause at your open door.
Can't help but see
the vase of flowers. A desk
that wasn't there before.
Someone's jacket
thrown across the chair.

Things come into this house
I know nothing about –
yet know like my own name
the squeak of the basement stair.
The contour of your Saturdays.
Where the pots are kept,
ready for summer geraniums.
I know how sunlight shifts
across each room, returning it
to shadow. What can be seen
looking out each window.

Looking in,
I withhold my knock.
See our kettle coming to boil
for tea in this chilled, uncertain
gloom. A new arrangement
on the coffee table. Your heel
as you leave the room.

CATHEDRAL HILL

I wake knowing you are awake
one neighborhood away. How restlessly
our failures haunt the night.
Yet outside your bedroom window
the silver-green light of the dome
redeems the whole neighborhood, unasked.

Here at my kitchen window
no earthly testimony interrupts the sky.
Though I can see clear to the moon,
after so many nights of clouds
I no longer know
if it is filling or emptying itself.

We stumble toward faith, you and I,
but have no language of deserving.
We have only our sleepless nights,
alone at our windows,
wondering what may lie ahead,
and who will be there.

At the Grocery

Weeks since our last good-bye
and I've no appetite.

My empty cart rattles past
apricots you'd have chosen
for their sun-gold skin,
kiwi's secret green, mangoes
whose thick rivers of juice
once lavished our chins.

I'm trying for something ordinary –

composure, let's say,
bread and butter,
common foods
inciting nothing.

But lifting an apple
one among the thousands

and holding its dead
weight

its lusterless
bruised
red

I stop

surrounded
by this pointless variety of fruit.

If you were here

you could tell me how to endure
having once been extraordinary
in your eyes.

IF YOU MUST BEGIN AGAIN

begin here

in silence

hold your
hungry self
in your own
loving arms

in the clearing
a wisp
of new moon
slips
from the grasp
of the trees'
dark inventory

look up

its contour
foreshadows
the fullness
that is to come

THIS CITY OF YOUR CHOOSING

City of possibility, of transiency,
sleeping on the couch of a friend of a friend,
living out of the trunk of the old Dodge.

City of want ads strewn across chipped linoleum,
a single plate and second-hand card table,
a single potato, a phone call for company.

City of windows open onto dusty sills and coos,
views of neighboring Peavey Park, its drifters
strewn in their repose across the day-worn grass.

City of nighttime sirens shrill and thrilling,
of street lights on storm-blown nights
flashing their yellow moons among the leaves

and above the tumult of restless branches,
above the rumble and honk and hunger,
the brazen clangs and clatters –

stars, faint but sure above this city of your choosing,
the same stars as from your childhood window –
the surprise of that, the extravagant assurance.

Since My Return from Nicaragua

I have been dreaming in Spanish.
A man shambles by, laden
with avocados for morning market.
Bicycles with girls on the handlebars
blur past in a Spanish whirl
of wheels and loosened phrases.

I'm back in the plaza of barter and chances,
coarse cotton blouses, the breezy
weave of sashes, smooth stones
for barefoot boys running,
shadows dense with history
where scavenging dogs slink.

I am borne by the jostling current
of aproned women among the harnessed
horses ribbed and listless. Heat shimmers,
unyielding as the poems of uprising
spray-painted night after night
on the walls of the old city
in the years when my country sent its guns.

Nicaraguita, I sing back to you
in the new tongue of dreams.
I've misplaced my own vocabulary
but do not miss the weight of it,
how its sharp edges dig into my back.

The air above us all –
Miskito, Mestizo, Español, Ingles –
throbs where our languages
have mixed, moist and turbulent,
gathering force for our daily drenching
of this universal, complicated rain.

THIS MAY NOT BE CORRECT

Approaching Taipei
we waken to the flight
attendant's dulcet voice:
Please distinguish your cigarettes.
Can you believe it? Back then

smoking was allowed on flights.
Fluids of many kinds were
graciously permitted. The world
was not yet proficient at fear.
Do I remember this correctly?

She glides up the aisle
with her bamboo basket
to welcome us to Asia.
*Would you like a hot trowel
for your face?* she offers

and we – charmed by this
custom, grateful for her effort
at our privileged language –
say *yes*, say *thank you* and
hold that balm of warmth
against our skin. Back then

before the internet pocketed
all our curiosity, we
learned about each other
directly, in simple gestures
of kindness given,
kindness received.

Half a World Away

Her backpack is light, even airy.
She studies maps, learns exchange rates.
Slips in a slim volume of Sara Teasdale
in case her native tongue might comfort.

He marvels, *Aren't you afraid?* meaning
Why can't you be more like me? Jokes,
Don't forget to come home. She won't

think of him at all while she's gone
until one night, half a world away,
alone in her shabby hotel,
she opens the volume and reads

Shall I be faithless to myself
Or to you?

And just that suddenly
she stands with all the women before her
who've known the price of either choice.
They open their hands to receive her
with sorrow, and with welcome.

WHEN WE FOUND OUT ABOUT THE BABY

You thrust our shovel
into a mound of spring snow
lingering in the shadow of the house.
Sprays of crystal shimmered
in wide arcs across the lawn,
flung in your harsh tempo
until all the fragments were laid bare
to melt. I turned
from the window.

For years I thought
you suffered less.
Now I see what men do.
They find a tool.
They wrap their fists around it.

LATE AFTERNOON, GULLS

The day we sat in our sweatshirts
at the café on the beach
and I said I felt invisible to you

you walked away
to search the shallows
for stones to skim across the silky water.
I watched you
weigh them in your palm
like each small need of my heart

then hurl them
like a boy
thinking to tame the menace of the depths.
You had a good arm.

Meanwhile, gulls picked through the trash
for meager nourishment. A child cried
because it was time to go.

Soon enough
the sun set on everything,
the stones sinking out of sight,
the burnished water turning to steel.

Bright Room with Linoleum Floor, 1993

I am nearing the end of obedience

class with my intractable

black lab who pulls

like our marriage

first one way, then

the same way, but harder.

I have a foreboding

about the final test –

the stretched leash

taut with our straining.

It Will End Like This

I'll be chopping vegetables for soup –
carrots, tomatoes, beans – the knife
you gave me deliberate in my hand.

I'll be making an effort again, not
because I'm happy, but because I'm not.
We have a pact.

Garlic will be crackling in the big red pot,
its aroma sharp, dependable.
This is the moment you will choose to tell me

you know by now it's over.
Your eyes will be blank, admitting nothing.
That's in the contract, too.

I won't cry out or touch you
but stand fully armed and helpless.

You will have come for this sign –
that I am unable to beseech you.

Then the final silence will have been uttered,
the shredding done, the searing of the throat.

LIKE THE BIRD

You, on the brink,
are you unsure

      if your trembling
      stems from thrill or fear?

Now that the known
has grown too thin

      go – let the world's magnitude
      take you in.

A bird does not interrogate
the unfamiliar sky

      but forsakes the nest
      there to belong

      feather, bone
      and song.

Be like the bird.
Fly

      to learn flight.

In Your Own Hands

I lived through it.
I took my time.

Night wind riffling the cottonwood
outside my open window

the kitchen corner where two walls met
and where I placed my forehead more than once

the headline posted on my refrigerator:
Scientists prove the body's supply of tears

is endless. "More bad news,"
I penciled in the margin

and went off to work. All of it
helped. Meanwhile the faithful moon

silvered my pillow. When I'd learned
enough my heart returned to me

whole and unashamed.

Let no one say you are not enough.
Let no one stop you from regarding your life

like a treasure, flawed but dear,
holding it up to the light

and turning it to radiance in your own hands.

3

Synchronizing the Heart

THE HEART WANTS YOU

to be happy

to settle comfortably
in every room of this life you've made

wants you to love those you love
without complication

but the heart, too,

knows the disquiet that dwells
in your deepest privacy

the restlessness that won't leave you

the heart waits for you
where you hesitate in the doorway

as if searching for a missing word

reveals
longings you don't know how to have

then claims it can't be held responsible
it's just your heart –

that thing you can't tame
that thing you'll do anything for

THE ART OF LONG AFFECTION

Sketched images fill your page, unfixed.
My hand, curled at rest.
Hair dangling

loose
as an afterthought.
Let each incompletion

suggest another facet,
your eye lingering on the still
unmapped

the tacit layers
of my geography.
Learn each small beauty

but tend also to the flaws –
the too-angular jaw, the gravity.
Soften their effects.

Trace my mouth,
my shoulder,
as if with your lips.

Draw me. Let your lines flow like rivers
penciled through the hills
of a needful country.

Let me be a study in your hands
so far from completion
as to be hardly begun.

WIDE OPEN

Here is the field we labor in together,
year after year rise to its rhythm –
the hoe, the horizon, our similar muscles,
the sweet, sweaty endlessness
of making our long mark on the earth.

We can be synchronized as sisters,
sway our hips to the jukebox tune,
rock each other's restless children,
tend to the soup pot, nurse the wounds.
We can demonstrate the methods of connection

and without pause be as brothers,
picture the room without certain walls,
rise for a hammer, a crowbar, and open
the house to the sound of crickets

laughing, and what if it rains?

We can write a long, strong story,
match our strides from memory,
walk into the clear, uncertain air of today
and live wide open, like surprise, like arms,
like the prairie unplowed.

COVENANT

This blunt darkness – yours –
let me attend

for in this life are we not meant
to carry each other

even in the staggering and spinning
even when words are not ready?

So surprisingly light
the small suitcase of certainty

left behind on the platform
as the train pulls away.

I am but one of many porters
and this is our bond:

while you are gone
(cocooned, disarranged)

your place remains at my table.
While you lie alone, as you must,

at night in your distant city,
your pulse beats in my wrist.

I can't explain it

but I am not afraid
to love you like this.

ABSENCE

Sleep   won't come
The soft
of my lips
is mine   alone
The hand
on my breast
my own
After hours   stillness
becomes   absence
stitched with sound
Rain   pebbling the roof
The frizz of wheels
on blue pavement
When the wind turns
restive
trees twist   and reach
and each bird
whose nest
is lost
must wait   with my heart
for morning
Sleep
sleep   won't come
won't   come

Aunt Grace

She was a little   strange.
Scared me sometimes

her talk of putting a brick
on my head so I'd never grow up

or squeezing me to pieces.
Could she? Smothering   affection

polyester bosom   ascetic shoes.
Small apartment for one.

Didn't drive. Didn't cook. Kitchen
cupboards stuffed with books.

Once, she said, God's thundering voice told her
she had no right to know about sex.

Was she lonely? More than the rest of us?
She took me on a Greyhound Bus

to Des Moines so I could say
I'd been somewhere.   I endured it.

Spent money she had too little of
on purses for me   trinkets

ceramic woodland animal babies.
By then   I was in college.

After she died   I dreamed
I heard the screen door   slap

and later found her wandering
in the alley   a light rain falling

on the hollyhocks and her upturned
face. In the end   there's only this:

Did I love her? Yes.
Did she know it?

DRAFT A LITTLE SOMETHING

There will come a troubled winter, ponderous with sludge
and snow, when you'll look out on the barren prospect
and know that your book will not be written,

that your collected works already have been collected
and even now are stacked to the rafters
in the hall closet of your striving, dust unto dust.

Bleakness will be heroic – perhaps everlasting –
the wan sunlight an admonishment
for planting seeds where none can flourish.

But then you may find yourself

pondering the word *wan* –
how it is similar to *want* and *wander*
and you'll feel the ancient quiver.

Use this moment wisely.
Reconsider your allegiance to self-doubt.
Inspect realism for its shortcomings.

Then draft a little something,
the fresh breeze of resolve blowing through you
in the old way, thrillingly, even wantonly.

Young Son, Sandwich Half-Eaten

When I had finished the cape
to your specifications – black,
reversible to gold lamé –
you swept it over your shoulders,
charged out back and dashed
across the deck to crush the foe.
How you flashed golden in the sun!
Then turned and leapt victorious
to the grass as you had done
a thousand times before
you had extra powers. Now
you could barely contain them
and bounded up the steps
with cardboard sword
to leap again and again.
I'm as big as the sky!
you shouted, and oh,
may it always be so,
I'm as big as the dark!

You Will Recall with Fondness Your Fifties

Rising each day to slip on responsibility like a pair of well-worn shoes.

Raising children – the utter fuss and ruckus of it.

Wholehearted toil without the follow-up heating pad.

Being seen as necessary.

Being seen.

An inventory of regrets, but still plenty of time to work on your personality.

The ambush of libido.

The view from the height of competence.

Jumping up to get going. Oh, you have no idea how much that will be missed.

Momentum.

Mortality in its grim little coat lingering on the far horizon where it belongs.

Knowing you won't ever have a studio in New York, but you still could.

THE ONES SHE SEEKS

Your mother eases past the stair,
fresh from her bath, uncertain where
the guest room is. She stares into the linen
closet until you come to guide her,
beneath your hand the surprise of skin

so soft as to be vanishing. For a while
you stand at her door then, before turning in.
Your mother has turned the heat way up
thinking it's the light switch. We twist
and throw the covers off all night, as in a fever.

When morning takes us off to work
your mother doesn't know where we have gone
though we leave yellow notes in the kitchen,
by her embroidery, tucked into *Reminisce*
and *Lutheran Life*. The house flutters with messages

but not the ones she seeks. She wanders upstairs
looking for a cat we've never had while our huge dog
waits forgotten by her chair. He's always there
to rest against her knee when she is sitting.
His brown eyes follow her up and down.

Your mother wants to be in heaven with her husband.
She thinks she's in Nepal. "*Saint* Paul, Mom."
Wherever this is, she says, she is content,
and doesn't wish to be any trouble. This is
her lifelong way of disappearing. And you

each day gather pieces of herself she misplaces,
tracking them like a trail of crumbs from childhood
that will lead you back to the mother you knew.
But when you tuck them in with her at night
you know they'll be gone by morning.

Someone's Grandmother Picks Up the Mail

She has taken her pills. Wiped the counters
clean. Clipped the coupons to her grocery list.
Responsibilities so small she is ashamed.

This is the shape of her loneliness now,
her mouth parched for lack of something to say.
Across the room, her husband emits a soft snore
from the recliner.

She pulls the silver key from the drawer
and sets out for the mailboxes downstairs.

Up and down the long hall
behind her neighbors' closed doors
hotdogs are coming to a pungent boil.

She could set her watch by it.

Rarely is there anything of interest or use
in the mail. She counts on achieving
that little disappointment each day before lunch.

So much comes at a person that is unwanted.
So much never comes.

MARY LOU'S KITCHEN

1

Our neighbors' house across the yard
you hold in high esteem
as the source of ice cream on sultry days
and nickels paid for necklaces made
of strung buttons, slipshod.
Your inventions feather their empty
nest. They've judged as best
your lightning-activated squirrel trap
with duct-taped curtain rod.

2

Today we step inside for a pre-demolition tour.
A pencil sketch and hammer grace the table
where a plate of cookies should be. Mary Lou
mentions dull cabinets and countertops.
Your eyes narrow in fealty to the familiar
until, shrewdly, she changes tack.

The first priority, she says, *is a bigger sink
to fill our new super-soakers.*
You blink with fresh respect.
*And we want more natural light
which means* (she lifts the hammer
in invitation) *this wall must come down.*

3

Oh, the glorious destruction. The manly strength
in your eight-year-old arms. Sheetrock dust drifts
onto your safety goggles and purple dinosaur shirt.
The pock-marked wall trembles with each blow
like a fortress collapsing under a barrage
of cannon fire and you, the cannon master.

Winded at last, the hammer at rest
on your thin shoulder, you grin
from the ruins. Have you ever been
happier? Did you have any idea
that this, alas, is how new things
sometimes must begin?

Un-doing

Let summer   be

Let bees' meandering
              teach you

the melody of breeze

After months
of winter shouldering
to the wheel

let light rain
              dissolve

your productivity

Let all your ends
              be loose

Let summer
              be

Into Your Singular Room

Soft around your shoulders like a shawl
you draw him

and he comes

unready, up-ended, to attend
his new calling and you, no matter how

bewildered.

He brings your meager groceries.
Hands you your cane.

He wants to say

> *Have I thanked you*
>
> *for your blood which formed me,*
> *for your milk and your wounds*
>
> *which furnished me?*

Afternoons of curled photos.
Laughter thinned by time

and apprehension. The patient

search for things discarded or misplaced
(a shoe, a name, sometimes affection).
Love letters. He thinks to himself

This is mine to you. I draw
near but not into your final privacy

where I rest my hand on your days.

EVERY KIND OF CLOUD

The vigil at his bedside stretches into stillness
like the solemn air of an August afternoon
leaden with the certainty of rain.
We are beyond language now.

At the window
I watch clouds form and shift, then drift
away. I love them as my father has.
Thank you, I say. The small 'o' of his mouth
shapes his shallow breath. We wait.
Night comes.

When next my father opens his eyes
he sees in a distant meadow
his mother and father, brothers, too,
alive again and waiting for him.
The food is ready. Ralph is still a boy,
chasing a mouse in the gilded grass.
My father quickens –

his eyes bright with a joke he remembers
playing or maybe has yet to play.
Paul is there too, strong and happy
like they were before the war. Looking up
he grins and calls to my father
Gordy, what took you so long?
The sky is filled with every kind of cloud.

She Wakes Me to See Fireflies

My friend and I
step off the farmhouse porch
into a snow-globe-swirl of light.
Tiny votive flames
carried by unseen pilgrims
swarm over the pasture
and up the flickering hills.
We shiver in our pajamas.

From the edge of the pond
frogs blurt
their unruly chorus.
The air is damp
with the exhalation
of cows.

In the cool sanctuary
of the country night
fireflies lift up
in their thousands.
The sky is speechless
with stars.

Rocket Pajamas

I love you more than outer space
my son murmurs
from his drift of blankets.

Tonight we talked about infinity,
so different from nothingness,
which he has deemed
the scariest thing, *not sharks,*
or a T-Rex, like some people think.

But I think as mothers do –
it's losing him. Torment of
nothingness – infinite wound –
if his scent should fade from the pillow – .
I send a thousandth silent prayer.

We wait. Our breathing slows and joins.
Stars begin to scatter their blossoms
across the field of night.

Now from the soft edge of sleep
his own conundrum resolves. *Infinity,*
he tells me, his voice blurred
but certain, *is like – everythingness.*
He closes his eyes, satisfied.

This universe beneath my hand, how is it mine to love?
Until now, what did I know of immensity?

CLIFF NOTES FROM YOUR MOTHER AS YOU LEAVE HOME

If it starts to spark, remove it.

The bigger mistake is not asking.

Don't wait too long to get started.

Drop every expectation that does not belong to you.

Always poke it first to see if it moves.

Sometimes the only method is inexperience.

Above all, be kind. No – be true to yourself. Also, kind.

If you're going to nap on the sofa, for heaven's sake tuck your glasses underneath it so you won't step on them when you get up.

Figure out for what you would walk through fire.

Walk through fire.

Terminal One

Airport traffic was insane, lanes
snarled, time compressed. I wedged
the Nissan into a slice of space,
adjacent cars in dizzying disorder
like those we saw on the unplowed
streets of northern Russia years ago.
Checked the rearview. Kept
the motor humming. We leaned across
the gearshift for an awkward hug
and laughed our good-byes.

Out you hopped. I popped
the trunk, you hoisted your bags,
drew out their long arms, waved
and rolled away. Why didn't I say
to hell with traffic, cut the motor,
come round the jutted bumper
to hold you a moment more?
It's one of a million things
I should have done

before you slipped away.

LETTER TO MY NIECES

I didn't have the work of you, or any daughter.
In the innocence of warm remove
I've read your lives, each biography
distilled, rough particulars filtered
to extract the essence –
strong spirits indeed.

You've taken photographs in Egypt,
the Tuscany hills, a Korean
classroom, Poland, Shanghai,
Uganda – places your foremothers
never imagined. Yet they, too,
explored the far country
of their possible selves, fierce
to stake a claim at the center
of their own lives
no matter who said *No*.

How deeply the world longs for women
to do this necessary thing.

I lift my grandmother's glass
to you – the familiar pattern etched
like female courage deep in the crystal –
and toast each departure without reserve.
For you are not mine, nor even ours, to hold
entangled in our roots. You are your own
itinerary, your own branch, leaf, splendor.

In the Beijing Alley Near Our Hotel

Children of the Beijing alley meat markets
fall asleep in their parents' cluttered stalls
among jumbled crates and plastic bags
listening to the chatter and chop of commerce.

The small ones drift awake from dreams of fish
and blood to meander pants-free in the open air
avoiding charcoal grills and motorbikes
and sharp-toothed eels wriggling in plastic buckets.

The child of the meat market knows how far to wander
without interference and where to find cooked
chicken to eat under the wooden tables
and which dogs to trust.

after Eileen O'Toole, *Dogs Who Love the Black Sea*

Suspended in the Air of China

Buckets dangling from construction cranes in the gap-
toothed skyline of Beijing.

Laundry flapping from thousands of hi-rise balconies across
Shanghai, where it is not permitted to hang laundry
from balconies.

A chicken coop affixed to an eighth-floor window.

Feathers.

A lone bird soaring over the Yangtze Dam, welcomed as a
sign that pollution is abating.

The rancid smell of yak butter burning in the lamps of
Lhasa's monasteries.

Cigarette smoke curling above the man astride an idling
motorbike, his pollution mask pulled down over his chin
while he smokes.

An empty seesaw in the train station plaza of Xi'an,
unintended consequence of the one-child policy.

Three undiscussables: Tibet, Taiwan, Tiananmen.

Purses hooked on tree branches in Luoyang's city square,
where women park their scooters on the way to work
and gather in the morning air to dance.

FISHING BOATS, YANGTZE

The woman ties knots,
sitting on an overturned bucket
beneath the canvas canopy.
The man steadies the rudder.
He squints at the silty water
and smokes. The motor chugs
its oily stench. Sometimes a child
peers up at us, our cameras.
How strange we are.

The fishermen's concrete villages
are clamped onto the steep slopes
of the flooded Seven Gorges.
Wooden steps scrabble down
hundreds of feet to the edge
of the Yangtze.

Last night
from the deck of our muscular ship
we saw the orange moon rise
and sit there.
The photograph is foolish –
a pinprick of light in a sea of black –
the wrong subject.

For days we drift along the surface
with our light luggage of wonder,
our prearranged questions
slowly refocusing as a lens does
from subject to field and back again

until what matters most is this
blurred background of tenderness
for the envoys of our common world.
Here: the fishermen's daughters
crouch on the shore barefoot
among the woven baskets,
their black hair spilling forward
as they wring out the day's laundry
in the lapping brown waters.

RETURNING HOME

We wake in our own bed on this side of the world
uncertain what ceiling this is,
muddled by travel.

We crave pickled eggs for breakfast for the first time.
Another oddity: all the lumbering blonde people
at the airport last night.

Yet how familiar, to draw clean water from the tap and brew
coffee instead of tea – how like a betrayal
it seems, carefree abandonment

of those we met – the Tibetan farmer in her rough kitchen,
the villager twisting Kleenex in her hands,
trembling as she spoke

of the Cultural Revolution. Schoolchildren for whom all that
is mere history, singing British rock songs to us
with a *stomp, stomp, clap!*

Stomp, stomp, clap! Black-clad elders we walked among as if
we meant to be friends, as if we felt we belonged
to a single human family.

For a while let me float between countries, like a bubble
that has mingled with other bubbles, touched
lightly, and lifted

into the borderless air. I want to believe there is no longer
a far side of the world. I want to remember
how easily

my heart can enlarge its membership.

PRECIPITOUS

1

The surgery on her brain went well
but damage had been building
since my mother didn't tell about her fall
(the bureau knob, the crack against the skull).
On the phone my brother said
we're to expect "precipitous decline."
Already she had told him how
the nurses moved her to a basement room
that crawled with giant bugs and snakes.
How she had called for help
but no one came.

2

I drove backward through time.
November drizzle smudged the broken fields,
then yielded to sleet that gloved with ice
each upturned stubble of corn.
What did I wish for now?

The road home glistened with new treachery
as darkness fell, then snow.

3

This morning (the town half-lidded,
glazed) culled branches litter streets
I used to know. I tiptoe to her room.
My mother's finger agitates the air.
Her eyes dart past, then fix on me
a feral wariness. She doesn't quite see
who I am, only her own distress.

Strange comfort in that familiar rule.
Across the alley
a downed power line sputters,
impotent and dangerous.

Just Out of Reach

My mother stands on the top rung of an aluminum ladder,
reaching for the manual typewriter on a shelf above her head.
I want to go to her but somehow can't. On this shelf

slumps the bulky accrual of her long life, dusty and worn.
The leather satchel from graduate school. The battered box
of homemade Halloween costumes unused in fifty years.

The lumpy green sleeping bag, its flannel lining cozy
against my legs one rainy morning in Illinois, Dad huddled
under the tent flap making pancakes on our camp stove.

She teeters. Certain things begin to make no sense. That we
got rid of those belongings when we moved her here. That she is
out of her wheelchair. That the nursing home allows her

to have a ten-foot ladder in her room. It occurs to me now
that she will fall. That she knows this danger but overrules it
with her urgency – so much yet to say – that this endeavor

may be a good enough way to die. She presses her lips
together, scoots the typewriter to the shelf's edge
and grunts, lifting it into her feeble arms. Of course

she tips back under its weight and *Oh!* – how unanswerable then
the thud of her body, the crack of her head, the reverberating clang
as the typewriter bounces and comes to rest on its side. Unmercifully,

this does not wake me. I want to go to her but somehow can't.
A good enough way I think in my panic, and though I am only
agreeing with her, immobile from the force of her own resolve,

and though it is only a dream, when I wake
the shame sticks to me all day, and even now.

I Push Her Wheelchair in the City of My Childhood

We bump across the lawn from the parking lot
to the entrance of the public gardens. Passing
feathered grasses and sentinel chrysanthemums
my mother comes face to face
with the puzzle of lingering autumn.

Almost Thanksgiving and she didn't want to come –
too cold, too much trouble – but now, sun struck,
blanket tucked around her, she murmurs *oh,* and *oh!*
at the profusion of purples, golds, lush greens
beyond all reason still thriving. Why so much, God?

Begonia, impatiens, verbena.
Common zinnias like she planted after the war.
She studies each sign. *Coleus,* I read aloud
and pause. My sister's favorite. *Cathy was just here,*
my mother guesses, though she was not.

I push again, her small weight heavy in the chair,
the wheels stubborn on the crinkled path. Soon
none of us will return to the city of our childhood.
For now, we are guests in the patient gardens.
Hibiscus, hydrangea, a triumph of wild rose.

My mother moves her lips, rummaging
for the words "annual," "perennial,"
though she never could keep them straight.
What lasts? she settles for asking
but I don't know how to answer.

A QUIET HOUR

Early morning and the lake is still.
Mist on the water shifts to veil,
then reveal, gulls adrift on the mirror.
In the chill air, sunrise is taking its
    sweet time.

I cannot remember everyone I have loved.
Every lake and tree, each uplifting
    solitude.
The household sleeps.
Nothing needs to be done

but to attend the imperceptible
    release
of night's remnant gray.
Shoreline rocks reclaim their essence.
A red kayak slips into the bay.

At last first sunlight sweetens
    the heart
of trees. Shadows withdraw
to their beds in the earth.
The sky is opening its gift of blue.

CATHY IN MY ROOM LAST NIGHT, SINGING

I heard Cathy in my room last night
singing, my mother confides,
speaking of my sister far away.
But I know she wasn't here.
She turns pleading eyes to me –

and I think of my son at three,
the earnest clamber into my lap
when the callous world confused him
and he trusted me to explain.

(This is life, my darling.
It's difficult sometimes. I'm sorry.)

Can we go upstairs now? my mother asks.
There is no upstairs here. No downstairs.
She was dressed all in white.

We sit in the falsely cheerful room
looking out at the blank lawn
waiting for something to happen,
something that will not be this.

Last Words

Did she speak this? –
        Did I dream it? –

dozing next to her
        in the dim light
        of the passage –

The world is so beautiful
so beautiful
        and has hurt so much

It is hard to let it go

BLESSING

Sorrow will come

May there also be kindness and grace

Easy silence in the place beyond words

and words to warm the silences

A channel that guards the passage

of your small and battered boat

then opens again, wide

WHAT THE PAINTER DARED IMAGINE

When old age comes
and memories merge

if your gallery of days
holds mainly impressionism

what pleasure! –
to be freed

to let your life be
what the painter dared imagine.

For is there not a beautiful authority

in the canvas that loosens
the strictures of accuracy

to confirm instead
                              radiance?

VARIED AND MARVELOUS THINGS

If one day you forget whether you have sung
the Brahms Requiem
still, you have sung it.

If you do not recall
every wedding, even so
there you danced.

You have synchronized your heart
with others' hearts
for causes both common and exalted

setting loose into the world
varied and marvelous things
that do not belong to you now.

They live in exquisite freedom
like children who've left home
to bless the world in their own way.

And did you not mean to lose yourself

in the work of beauty
pouring its thimbleful
into the ocean of human endeavor?

No more would you call
your children back
into your body

than ask which shell is yours,
which fragment of spray,
shimmer, salt.

ACKNOWLEDGEMENTS

Thank you to the editors of the following publications, in which several of these poems first appeared, sometimes in different versions or with different titles:

ArtWord Quarterly: "Potato Man"
Autumn Sky Poetry Daily: "The Warm Lap of September"
Bird's Thumb: "Just Out of Reach"
By&By: "The Kind of Thing We Did"
Cairns Arts Journal: "Since My Return from Nicaragua"
damselfly press: "Into Your Singular Room"
Minnesota Monthly: "Sitting in Lawn Chairs After a Complicated Day" and "When We Found Out About the Baby"
Page and Spine: "Terminal One" and "Wide Open"
Red Wolf Journal: "The Heart" and "Photograph"
Talking Stick: "Bright Room with Linoleum Floor, 1993" and "This New Arrangement"
Tishman Review: "Late Afternoon, Gulls"
Wilderness House Review: "Cathy in my Room Last Night, Singing," "How the Swedes Eat Grapefruit," "In Your Own Hands," and "What There Is to Remember"

About the Author

Marg Walker is a lifelong writer who pursues her abiding interest in the human voice through poetry, creative nonfiction, and choral music. During her professional career as a consultant, Marg specialized in narrative inquiry as a source of learning for foundations and nonprofits working in the human services and the arts. She is a member of Unity Singers, an a cappella ensemble, and has collaborated with choral artists to create programs of music and poetry. Marg's poems have appeared in numerous publications, and a few lucky poems have been chosen by composers to be transformed into song. Marg has one adult son. She lives with her husband in St. Paul, Minnesota.